1000 Resumes, One job...
...an Employer's Perspective

About the Author

Phil Peretz is a business owner and entrepreneur who has spent his entire life in business. At 14, he was a freelance photographer for the Oakland Times and a restaurant manager in the Rockridge district in Oakland at 16.

Out of school, his professional career starting off in advertising as a classified advertising manager for a series of weekly papers, then as an art director, retail operations manager, sales manager and VP of sales in both the printing and high tech industries.

9 years of his career was with Kinko's where he started off as a very successful sales rep for the Berkeley, CA territory and went on to be promoted to Regional Sales Manager, Director of Sales and then Regional Sales VP.

Peretz currently lives in Reno Nevada where he and his wife, Catherine Young-Peretz, own Media Media Inc. and is co-owner of Nationwide Barcode.

Throughout his career, Peretz has been responsible for the interviewing and hiring of several hundred employees. He brings his personal experiences to life with this book in the hopes of coaching people to find the career they desire.

Phil Peretz
© 2011 Phil Peretz, Media Media Inc. - All Rights Reserved
www.mediamediainc.com
phil@mediamediainc.com

Table of Contents

You and the Pareto Principle.

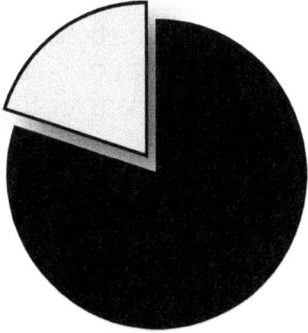

The Pareto principle, also known at the 80-20 rule, the vital few or the principle of factor sparsity states that 80% of the effects come from 20% of the causes.

Business management thinker Joseph Juran suggested this principle and named it after Italian economist Vilfredo Pareto who observed in 1906 that 80% of the land was owned by 20% of the population.

He further developed the principle by observing that 20% of the pea pods in his garden contained 80% of the peas. Business people have taken this further and acknowledge that 20% of the customers bring in 80% of the revenue and 20% of a sales team bring in 80% of the business.

In manufacturing, 80% of your inventory will come from 20% of your suppliers, 20% of your inventory takes up 80% of the space, 20% of the staff will create 80% of the problems, There have been studies that 20% of the population use 80% of health care resources, 80% of the crimes are committed by 20% of the criminals, etc.

Depending on what you are looking at and how you are categorizing it, you can use the Pareto principle to identify both the critically good and the critically bad.

Over the last few years, businesses have laid off a lot of people. The truth is, they laid off the bottom 20-50% of their staff. Since it became okay for businesses to let everyone know that they were downsizing, right-sizing or reorganizing, this was a perfect opportunity to get rid of the people who were not performing.

The majority of business managers, owners and executives have been exposed to this rule at some point in their career and they believe in it. It's up to you to prove to them during your entire term of employment that you are in the smaller percentage of employees who contribute to the larger percentage of results.

In your job search, you want to be one of the amazingly great...the vital few. You want to demonstrate that you are one of the 20% who will achieve the 80%.

Everything you do, your approach, your resume, your conversations, your manner of speech and the way you dress for the interview has to be top-notch. You have to demonstrate that you are the best candidate for the company. If you are not, you will not get hired.

The Law of Opportune Timing

As long as the human race has existed, most people have believed that their lives are controlled by God, fate or some strange mystical outside force. To increase their good fortune, people have visited fortune tellers, seers, astrologers, priests, shaman, prayed to God, gods or other deities, tossed yarrow sticks, read the Bible, Torah, Talmud, I-Ching or Tarot cards, and consulted mystics and gypsies.

Although a belief system is a wonderful thing, our inordinate faith in ourselves and our abilities must be a part of it. We need to develop processes that we can use continuously to improve ourselves. Whether you believe that "God helps those who help themselves" or you believe in the approach of tapping into divine energy and you create your own fortune, this is the Law of Opportune Timing. Fortune is the result of doing the right things at the right time.

The author Steven Covey tells a story about two lumberjacks who were competing to see who could chop down the most trees. The first lumberjack worked hard all day long, scarcely even stopping to eat a bite of lunch. It seemed sure he would win the contest. He observed that the other lumberjack was stopping almost every hour and sitting down for several minutes.

At the end of the day he lost the contest. He asked the other lumberjack, "How could that be?"

The other lumberjack replied, "Did you notice that every time I was sitting down, I was sharpening my saw?" This allowed his to sharpen the saw and be more efficient while working. As a result, he was able to get more work done in the same amount of time.

Sharpening the saw refers to improving ourselves. In order to be prepared for events and people that come into our lives, we must be receptive and we must be constantly sharpening the saw and adding to our skills and abilities.

What skills do you have where you excel? Do you take the time out of your day to improve yourself? Are you in the top 20%?

It doesn't matter whether you are in sales, administration, customer service, finance or management; the outcome is really the same. You are there to add to the profitability of the company. By doing things, better, faster, more efficiently, you have the ability to do this for your employer at any level of an organization. When you can prove this to your employer, you become a valuable member of the team and almost impossible to replace.

Let's start off by with personal assessment and then, we'll move into goal setting....but, first things first.

First things First

You need a job. Businesses need to make money. They make money by having products and services that people need or want. Ideally, they have smart, well trained, friendly employees educating customers why they should buy from them. Ideally, you work for them.

So, how do you get the job? Simple...you have to demonstrate to the employer that you will make an impact. You have to be able to look at things from their perspective and work at being an asset of their organization. You have to make a difference.

Over the last 30 years or so, I have looked at thousands of resumes. I have hired hundreds of people as a direct supervisor, a hiring manager or influencing manager. I know what makes a great candidate and a great employee, and I have been on the other side of the desk. I have applied for many different positions since I was a teenager. I've convinced people to hire me in spite of not having a college degree. I have been hired over MBAs because I have identified how I could fit into an organization. I have been able to look at situations and find the ways that I could help them make money. I have always looked for things that would set me apart from everyone else and then promoted my strengths. You can do this too.

Granted, there are a lot of positions that require a degree, but if you do not have one, don't let that keep you from finding a job. A lack of a degree limits your choices in certain areas, but there are lots of opportunities. In fact, Bill Gates (Microsoft) and Larry Ellison (Oracle) don't have college degrees.

This book will give you some insights as to what managers look for, how to capture their attention and the things you can do to position yourself as a top contender for the job you desire.

This economy and the lay-offs created a situation where there are hundred, even thousands of people all going after the same position.

I met Jim Cathcart several years ago at a training exposition in Atlanta. Although I had just met him in person, I've always been a fan of his. Jim has written many books, including *The Acorn Principle*, *Relationship Selling* and more recently, *The Eight Competencies of Relationship Selling*.

He is a professional speaker and a Toastmaster's International Golden Gavel Award Winner. His passion is personal development and cultivation and his mantra is...

"How would the person I'd like to be...
...do the things I'm about to do?"

This single thought can lead to a great deal of personal evolution and improvement.

None of us wake up in the morning and tell ourselves that we want to fail. There are, however, many things in the course of the day, especially if you are unemployed, that will cause negativity and self-doubt. Hopefully, when you go through this process, you are in a positive and open minded frame of mind.

So, who is it that you'd like to be? Director of Marketing? HR Manager? Receptionist? Administrative Assistant? Customer Service Rep? How would THAT person do the things that you are about to do?

How would he or she initiate contact?
How would they sound on the phone when they had the phone interview?
At the interview, how would that person dress and act?
What questions would he or she have for the interviewer?
How would he or she follow up?

Why should they hire you out of all of the people who have applied for the position?
How will you make a difference?

The purpose of this book is to help you get motivated, stay motivated, learn what hiring managers are looking for, to stay focused and get a job...or, a better job.

Let's have some fun!

Here are a couple of websites that have quick quizzes to help you to open your mind to some different career choices based on your personality.

http://www.ivillage.co.uk/what-career-will-suit-your-personality/121527
http://www.selectsmart.com/topjobs.html

Be sure to type in the web addresses exactly as above.

Sometimes it's a good idea to think about other careers or types of jobs that you can go after using your transferable skills. We'll be discussing transferable skills in a few chapters.

The Three As

Attitude, Aptitude and Appetite

You probably think that you need 'them' more than they need you. You may be feeling anxious and a little less confident than usual.

You are going to spend a lot of time trying to impress hiring managers. It's a lot of work, but there will be a pay-off. You will find a job, you will increase your income and you will be better off.

Regardless of the position in a company, the outcome is the same. Every person in every company, regardless of their position, has the same bottom line function...to help grow the company and facilitate profits.

It's up to you to take a personal assessment, put it on paper (your resume), convince the hiring manager that you have the needed skills and convince them that you can be an asset. You need to convince them that they need you and you will be a valuable member of their organization.

You have skills and they need profits.

It's a trade. If you can prove to the employer that you can add to their profitability, they will hire you. There is a good chance that if you do this right, they will hire you whether or not there is a posted position for an employee.

It's up to you to demonstrate that you can do this and the best way is by showing them that you have the three A's.

ATTITUDE - a cheerful, friendly, positive frame of mind with good presence and a high, yet realistic, confidence level.

APTITUDE is much more than formal education. It is a capacity and desire for learning.

APPETITE - the pure desire to succeed and willingness to do what it takes to accomplish it.

There was a book that I read several years ago that discussed two types of people:

People who play to **win**, and people who play to **not lose.**

People who play to **win** do so with a tremendous amount of spirit and are risk takers. People who play to **not lose** tend not to take chances, tend not to get noticed and consequently, tend not to be as successful as the people who play to win. The moral: as you go out to find that new job, play to win.

There are a lot of people competing against you, be the winner! You need to be the winner for your sake and for the people counting on you to succeed.

What are your strengths?

One of the most important processes that a person can go through is an inventory of personal strengths and skills. Once identified, you will be able to project these strengths to others in a resume, cover letter and in the interview. Being familiar with your strengths translates to your having personal confidence.

Once you take an inventory of the strengths you have, you will understand what makes you special...what makes you valuable.

The purpose of this process is to give yourself an accurate self-assessment of your abilities. Then you will translate this assessment into the words that you will use to describe yourself and tie those to the needs of a business.

The areas where you feel that you have weaknesses are those areas where you should commit to improving. You will focus on your strengths and will downplay your areas of improvement.

Some of your strengths have been gained from on the job experiences, some are from hobbies, school, home or military service.

We'll go into detail after the assessment on the next page.

The next two pages have a list of skills. Next to each of the traits are a circle ○ and a square ❑
If you possess the skills, put a checkmark over the circle, if you need to develop or expand these skills, put a checkmark over the square.

Transferable Skills

- ○ ❑ Meet deadlines
- ○ ❑ Ability to delegate
- ○ ❑ Ability to plan
- ○ ❑ Results oriented
- ○ ❑ Customer Service oriented
- ○ ❑ Supervises others
- ○ ❑ Ability to increase sales
- ○ ❑ Ability to increase efficiency
- ○ ❑ Accepts responsibility
- ○ ❑ Able to instruct others
- ○ ❑ Desire to learn
- ○ ❑ Desire to improve
- ○ ❑ On-time/punctual
- ○ ❑ Good time management
- ○ ❑ Problem solving skills
- ○ ❑ Manage money or budgets
- ○ ❑ Enjoys meeting the public
- ○ ❑ Manage people
- ○ ❑ Organize people
- ○ ❑ Organize projects
- ○ ❑ Team player
- ○ ❑ Good presentation skills
- ○ ❑ Good written communications
- ○ ❑ Works in groups
- ○ ❑ Works independently
- ○ ❑ Computer Skills

Working with Information/Data

- ○ ❑ Can analyze data or facts
- ○ ❑ Good investigation skills
- ○ ❑ Audit Records/Books
- ○ ❑ Keep Financial Records
- ○ ❑ Locate answers or information
- ○ ❑ Classify data
- ○ ❑ Count, observe, compile

- ○ ❑ Research
- ○ ❑ Detail oriented
- ○ ❑ Take inventory
- ○ ❑ Math skills

Working with people

- ○ ❑ Patient
- ○ ❑ Nurturing/Care for
- ○ ❑ Persuasive
- ○ ❑ Able to confront others
- ○ ❑ Pleasant
- ○ ❑ Counsels people
- ○ ❑ Sensitive
- ○ ❑ Can demonstrate an item or idea
- ○ ❑ Supportive
- ○ ❑ Diplomatic
- ○ ❑ Public speaking skills
- ○ ❑ Helps others
- ○ ❑ Tactful
- ○ ❑ Insightful
- ○ ❑ Ability to teach or mentor
- ○ ❑ Interview skills
- ○ ❑ Anticipates needs
- ○ ❑ High energy
- ○ ❑ Open minded
- ○ ❑ Kind
- ○ ❑ Takes orders from others
- ○ ❑ Good listening skills
- ○ ❑ Serving
- ○ ❑ Trust
- ○ ❑ Works with others
- ○ ❑ Negotiating skills
- ○ ❑ Understanding
- ○ ❑ Adaptable
- ○ ❑ Outgoing

Using Words or Ideas
- ○ ❑ Articulate
- ○ ❑ Innovative
- ○ ❑ Strong verbal skills
- ○ ❑ Logical
- ○ ❑ Remembers information
- ○ ❑ Accuracy
- ○ ❑ Research
- ○ ❑ Create new ideas
- ○ ❑ Analytical

Using Words or Ideas (continued)
- ○ ❑ Design ability
- ○ ❑ Public Speaking – small settings
- ○ ❑ Public Speaking – medium groups
- ○ ❑ Public Speaking – large groups
- ○ ❑ Writes clearly
- ○ ❑ Detail oriented

Leadership skills
- ○ ❑ Arranges social functions
- ○ ❑ Motivates people
- ○ ❑ Negotiates agreements
- ○ ❑ Decisive
- ○ ❑ Plans
- ○ ❑ Delegates
- ○ ❑ Runs meetings
- ○ ❑ Directs others
- ○ ❑ Explains things to others
- ○ ❑ Self-motivated
- ○ ❑ Gets results
- ○ ❑ Share leadership
- ○ ❑ Thinks of others
- ○ ❑ Directs projects
- ○ ❑ Team builder
- ○ ❑ Solves problems
- ○ ❑ Mediates problems
- ○ ❑ Takes risks
- ○ ❑ Empowers others

Creative/Artistic
- ○ ❑ Artistic
- ○ ❑ Music appreciation
- ○ ❑ Design skills
- ○ ❑ Dance, body movement
- ○ ❑ Draw, sketch, render
- ○ ❑ Presents artistic ideas
- ○ ❑ Plays instruments
- ○ ❑ Expressive

Other Skills

○ ☐ _____
○ ☐ _____
○ ☐ _____
○ ☐ _____
○ ☐ _____
○ ☐ _____
○ ☐ _____
○ ☐ _____
○ ☐ _____
○ ☐ _____
○ ☐ _____
○ ☐ _____
○ ☐ _____
○ ☐ _____
○ ☐ _____
○ ☐ _____
○ ☐ _____
○ ☐ _____
○ ☐ _____
○ ☐ _____
○ ☐ _____
○ ☐ _____
○ ☐ _____
○ ☐ _____
○ ☐ _____
○ ☐ _____
○ ☐ _____
○ ☐ _____
○ ☐ _____
○ ☐ _____
○ ☐ _____
○ ☐ _____
○ ☐ _____
○ ☐ _____
○ ☐ _____
○ ☐ _____
○ ☐ _____
○ ☐ _____
○ ☐ _____
○ ☐ _____
○ ☐ _____

Notes

If you have gained your skills at home, school, in the military, as a volunteer or on the job, you should be able to take those skills and apply them to your future job positions even if the work appears to be somewhat unrelated to your past employment or education.

Your transferable skills can be much more important that job-related skills. When you are changing jobs, careers or making the move from school to your first job, it's important to focus more on your overall transferable skills.

> *Transferable skills are those skills that can be used in many different occupations, regardless of the type of job. They are universal skills and are the common denominator between your experiences and your future job. You can transfer them from one job to another with little or no effort on your part and without any additional training from your employer.*

If you are a graphic designer wanting to move into web design and your last job was designing catalogs, you should emphasize general design skills, not the specific print skills. If you have been a nanny and you want to move into child care, you would focus of the activities relating to the care of children along with time management. Same with an automotive mechanic would wants to move into a maintenance position. He would go into detail about general repair and mechanical skills, not the specific skills as it related to fixing cars.

Transferable Skill

Example

Connection

The previous pages covered a number of 'top-level' skills. Your skills are both what you have learned on-the-job and those that you have gained from day-to-day living. Many job seekers overlook their own potential. These skills can put you in a position to meet or exceed a potential employer's expectations.

Now that you are thinking about this in more detail, go

back and finish the worksheet adding anything that you may have overlooked. Once you have identified these skills, you need to start thinking about how to turn them into statements that will show your future employer that you have the 3 As.

Transferable skill: Directs others
Example: While in school, I was consistently the team leader for group projects
Connection: If I was able to do this in school, I will also be a go-to person as I gain more knowledge about this position with your company.

Transferable Skill: Computer Skills
Example: I am computer savvy with Word, Works, Excel, Access, and Powerpoint.
Connection: I have used Windows-based programs for the last 10-years. This will mean that I need no training on commercial programs and minimal training on any job-specific computer programs

Transferable skill: Well organized
Example: I reported to 4 different people at my last job
Connection: I am able to work with solid and dotted line reporting structures and maintaining my composure. This required that I had to organize my time and set priorities to satisfy everyone's needs. I'm sure that I can easily handle the organizational demands of this position.

Transferable skill: Public speaking skills
Example: On the debate team in high school
Connection: I spent two years on the debate team in my high school speaking on a variety of topics. This gave me the confidence and training to speak in front of individuals and groups of people without hesitation. I would be a perfect customer service representative for your company since I have these skills.

The next page has a worksheet to help you go through this as an exercise.

Transferable Skill: _____

Example: _____
Connection: _____
_____
_____
_____

Transferable Skill: _____

Example: _____
Connection: _____
_____
_____
_____

Transferable Skill: _____

Example: _____
Connection: _____
_____
_____
_____

Transferable Skill: _____

Example: _____
Connection: _____
_____
_____
_____

Transferable Skill: _____

Example: _____
Connection: _____
_____
_____
_____

Transferable Skill: _____

Example: _____
Connection: _____
_____
_____
_____

Transferable Skill: _____

Example: _____
Connection: _____
_____
_____
_____

Transferable Skill: _____

Example: _____
Connection: _____
_____
_____
_____

Transferable Skill: _____

Example: _____
Connection: _____
_____
_____
_____

Transferable Skill: _____

Example: _____
Connection: _____
_____
_____
_____

Setting Goals

Keep Goals Simple and **SMART.**

Specific: Well defined - clear to understand.
Measurable: Know if the goal is obtainable and know when it has been achieved
Agreed Upon: Agreement with all people involved. You have to believe that you can do it – if you have a spouse/partner/children, they need to give you the space and support to do this.
Realistic: Within the availability of resources, knowledge and time
Time Based: Enough time to achieve the goal but not so much time that you will cool off from achieving this goal.

To quote renowned American philanthropist Elbert Hubbard:

> *"Many people fail in life, not for lack of ability or brains or even courage, but simply because they have never organized their energies around a goal."*

While you are in the job-searching process, it's important to think of goal setting in terms of activity goals and broad-based goals.

Good goals would include:

- I will contact 10 companies in my area, in person, every day for the next 7 days.
- I want to get a job as a (salesperson, customer service rep, auto mechanic, VP of Finance, etc.) at a medium size company in my area within the next 90 days.
- I will set up 4 interviews for a Customer Service position with businesses in my area every day for the next 7 days starting on January 3rd of this year.
- I will send out 20 resumes a week to companies for the position of accounts payable during the next 4 weeks.

Ineffective Goals are:

- I will get a job as store manager at Safeway on Main Street.
- I want a job.
- I will call companies within a 3 mile radius to get an interview.
- I will look at the classifieds in my local paper every day.

These goals are ineffective because they are open-ended. When you set an open-ended goal, you haven't met the criteria of having a SMART goal.

The next page has a basic worksheet with examples and the following page has a blank worksheet that you can photocopy and use.

Goal Setting

GOALS					
Goal	**Specific**	**Measurable**	**Agreed**	**Realistic**	**Time**
What do you want to achieve?	Well defined - easy to understand	Is the goal measurable? (y/n)	Do you believe in this goal? (y/n)	Do you have resources, knowledge & time (y/n)	By When? (00/00/0000 format)

Action Steps
1.
2.
3.
4.

Goal #1

Write my resume.	Write two versions of my resume. One for customer service and one for inside sales.	Yes	Yes	Yes	1/1/0000

Action Steps
1. Go to Barnes and Noble to buy a resume writing book for reference
2. Write basic resume to be used for both versions
3. Create two versions – customer service and inside sales
4. Go to Office Max – print 250 of each (buy matching envelopes and get extra paper for cover letters)

Goal #2

Find a job	Receptionist making a yearly salary of minimum $32k for a mid size company.	Yes	Yes	Yes	3/15/0000

Action Steps
1. Contact 75 companies a week by phone/in-person – get name of hiring manager
2. Contact each hiring manager in order to send a resume and cover letter
3. Send a minimum of 25 resumes
4. Follow up 5 days after resume was sent – set-up minimum of 6 interviews a week
5. Send Thank you cards after interview.

GOALS

Goal	Specific	Measurable	Agreed	Realistic	Time
What do you want to achieve?	Well defined - easy to understand	Is the goal measurable? (y/n)	Do you believe in this goal? (y/n)	Do you have resources, knowledge & time (y/n)	By When? (00/00/0000 format)

Goal #___

Action Steps

1.

2.

3.

4.

Goal #___

Action Steps

1.

2.

3.

4.

Goal #___

Action Steps

1.

2.

3.

4.

Starting the Job Search

You are reading this because one of two things is taking place:
- You are unemployed and are looking for a job - or -
- You are employed and you are looking for another job.

Either way, you are going through a stressful transition in your life. Although it may not feel like it right now, you are on the brink of a new adventure. Good luck!

Here are several handy tips as you prepare:

1. Create a Vision Board. There is a power in visualizing what you are going to achieve. Stay focused and program your subconscious to succeed. A vision board is a collage of words and pictures that depict your goals. Here is a great article on creating a vision board. http://www.ehow.com/how_4494911_make-vision-board.html

2. Turn to friends, family, and contacts that you have made over the years. If you have been a business professional, you've built up a database or address book. Use it. Ask those contacts if they know anyone who may hire you.

3. Surround yourself with positive people who will give you confidence and strength. Stay away from anyone who is not supportive and positive.

4. Your job search IS your job. Set up an office in your home to handle this business of finding a job. Eliminate distractions and stay motivated. Anticipate and avoid anything that will keep you from finding a job. If there are positive things in your life that you have been doing prior to this job search - going to church, school, the gym - keep doing them! Spend as much time as you can each day looking for companies that may hire you. This time should be devoted to uninterrupted job searching duties. No personal incoming or outgoing calls. You can always return calls later. Learn to terminate a discussion - this is a very important transferable skill. Anytime the phone rings, answer professionally. It may be your next employer.

5. Know yourself, your strengths and your weaknesses. Work to improve your weaknesses and make them your strengths. Never

think that self-improvement is a finite process. You can always improve yourself, and your job search.

6. Do not think you completely control your job search. Be alert to chance. There is something to be said about being in the right place at the right time. Your job is to be in as many of those right places as possible.

7. Your job search does not end with your next job. Always have another goal to work towards and your career will continue to advance, even in difficult times.

8. Keep a diary of all resumes sent, all appointments and activities as it relates to your search.

9. Research! Find out as much as possible about the companies that you are interested in.

   You are doing several things:
   a. Gaining knowledge in order to demonstrate that you care about the company.
   b. Gaining knowledge in order to make an educated decision as to whether or not you want to work there.
   c. Building transferable skills. Everything that you are learning can be used for the next interview.

10. Manage Social Networking.

Managing Social Networking

The internet has made the world a very small place.

Go to Google, Yahoo or Bing, type in your full name and see what comes up.

When search for myself, there are links to posts that I made all the way back in the early 90s, there are links to my MySpace page that I haven't used in several years, links to Facebook, LinkedIn, businesses that I own or owned, businesses that I have managed or worked for. Frankly, it's frightening.

Your on-line life and internet history is right there for people to see.

Interviewers and prospective employers can and will see a lot of your history in a matter on minutes.

They can learn how you talk, act, think, who you associate with and whether the information on your resume matches your internet history

If you look at the screenshot, you'll see a reference to my being a Director of Sales for Speedway Copy Systems. I left this position in 2000 and it still shows up. On subsequent pages, there are press releases that I posted when I was a Sales Manager for Kinko's in 1993. The internet has a long memory and it's critical that you spend some time positioning or repositioning yourself.

Next, take a look at all of your social networking sites and make sure that your posts are positive or at least neutral.

Religious and political fanaticism on either side of the spectrum can keep you from getting hired. Constant misspellings or poor grammar in your posts will lead the reader to think that you are sloppy. Photos or posts about drinking or drugs and photos that can be taken wrong or are too revealing will definitely keep you from getting hired.

Hiring Managers have to make the best decisions for their company and if your internet reputation makes you look like you are a bad risk, they will make that decision to not hire you without asking for your input.

Is this fair?

Absolutely yes! Ask yourself what you would do if you were responsible for a business and the productivity of a group of employees. You would surround yourself with the best people that you could trust.

As you are looking to promote yourself during your job search, you are bringing your best to the position. You don't want forgotten or foolish things to be the reason you are passed over. It is critically important that you focus on reputation management and delete anything in your social networking sites that may be misconstrued and is not in alignment with your resume and your goals.

Don't assume that privacy settings will keep your information private. Do assume that everyone has access to your online history.

Remember: Make sure your internet history and your resume match.

Your e-mail address

Your e-mail address says a lot about you.

Your e-mail address is one of the first things that employers see on your resume and they will be quick to form an opinion.

Comcast, MSN and especially AOL e-mail addresses tend to tell people that you are not very computer savvy. Except for having your own domain name, Google e-mail addresses are the best and under no circumstance should you be sending out email on your existing or previous bosses e-mail domain or a family or friend's email address.

Your e-mail address should be as neutral as possible. The preferred e-mail address would be first.lastname@google.com. Other variations are first initial and last name, first initial, middle initial and last name. Sometimes this is very difficult in the case of common first and last names, but with some experimenting, you will find a good email address.

Under no circumstances should you ever use an email address that includes references to music, movies, TV, sex, drugs, politics or religion.

Silly e-mail addresses indicate a level of inappropriateness and will keep you from being considered.

Bootylicious@email.com, weedman420@email.com, spoiledprincess@email.com, redneck2020@email.com and treehugger4life@email.com don't get called. (I've modified these examples, don't try to e-mail them)

Getting a Google e-mail address will take you about 5 minutes.

The Sales Process

Finding a job is sales. It's a very strategic and multi-part process.

Whether you are selling high tech instrumentation, real estate, professional services or you are looking for a job, the sales cycle is always the same.

There are three major parts:
- Planning and Prospecting
- Qualifying, Presenting and Gaining Commitment.
- Follow Up.

Planning and Prospecting

Market Qualification
Pre-Call Planning

Qualifying, Presenting and Gaining Commitment

Building Rapport	Determining Needs
	Presentation
	Gain Commitment
Follow up	

Planning and Prospecting
1. Market Qualification
    a. Is the job you are looking for out there?
    b. How can you fit into the current available job market?
    c. Are there any skills that you need to develop or improve in order to find this job?

2. Pre-Call Planning
    a. Get your resume and coversheet in order
    b. What industries and what businesses should you call on?
    c. Research the company or companies where you have interest.
    d. Who do you need to talk to?

Qualifying, Presenting and Gaining Commitment
This is where you start presenting yourself to the employers.

1. Determining Needs
    a. Do they need you?
    b. Do you want to work for them?
    c. Could this be a good fit?

2. **Present Solutions/Make Presentation**
    a. Get face to face with the hiring manager.
    b. Your interview IS your presentation. Although the hiring manager has a series of questions for you, it is very important that you present all of the reasons that you want to work there. This is also the time to ask enough questions so you will know that you are on the right employment path.

3. **Gain Commitment**
    a. Get a commitment for either a second interview and/or be a continuing part of the hiring process. Rarely do people hire on the spot. Here is where you get a commitment to take this hiring process to the next level.

Follow Up
1. After you have gained commitment, following up to close the sale is critically important. This is the time that you demonstrate the appetite portion of the 3-As.

Gaining and Building Rapport
This entire book is about building value which is the cornerstone building rapport. Here are some other tips.

1. Introduce yourself when you meet.

2. Have your potential employer's best interests at heart. This is an opportunity to show your future employer that you are valuable.

3. Establish eye contact. -- This is important - when talking to someone hold their gaze for about 5-10 seconds. Any longer than this can seem creepy or odd so break the gaze by looking off to the side or slightly above their head. Don't look down as this may indicate the end of your conversation or a sudden lack of confidence. Try it now. Hold your head still and think about the last time you did something or went somewhere. You will notice that your eyes may move up or to the side. When your listener sees this, they will think that you are remembering something and will continue to listen to you.

4. Relate, don't lecture. When you speak, make it conversational. Don't give a speech or a narrative. Find out what's important to them (as it regards their business). Have your resume memorized, have examples how you have helped your previous employer and how it

will relate to them when they hire you. If you used acronyms or terms that were specific to your last job, don't use them unless you can explain them immediately.

5. Dress appropriately.

6. Avoid using humor or language that might offend them. Toastmasters International™ suggests avoiding language or topics best left in the "bathroom, barroom, or bedroom." Also avoid stereotypes of all sorts.

The Hiring Process

There are only two possibilities that take place in the hiring process.

- There is already an open position –or-
- You have convinced the company that they have a need and you are the solution. If you can do this, you have no competition. You've demonstrated the 3 As and you have shown that you can help solve a problem that exists within their company.

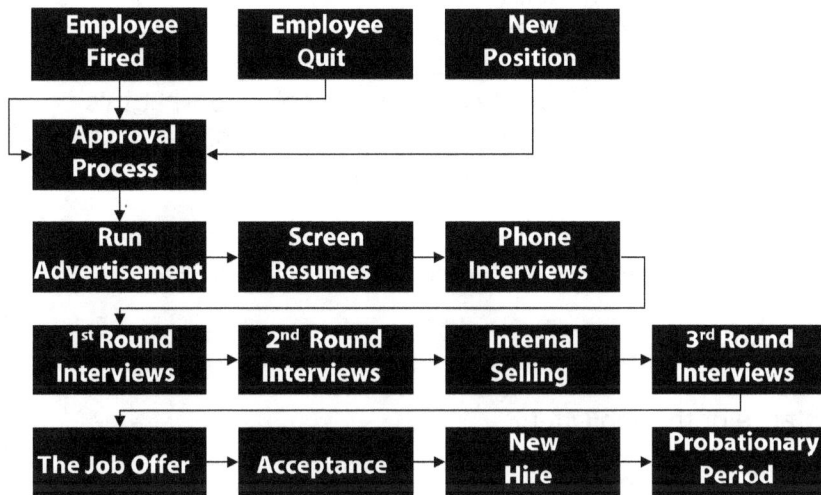

Employee Fired	Employee Quit	New Position	
Approval Process			
Run Advertisement	Screen Resumes	Phone Interviews	
1st Round Interviews	2nd Round Interviews	Internal Selling	3rd Round Interviews
The Job Offer	Acceptance	New Hire	Probationary Period

When there is an existing need, there are three possible scenarios that took place

- An employee was fired.
- An employee quit.
- A new position was created.

For the purpose of describing the hiring process, let's take a look at what happens when an employee is fired or has quit.

- The manager creates a hiring profile and writes a help-wanted ad to replace the employee who is leaving. Usually they turn to the direct supervisor for final approval or consensus. In larger companies the Human Resources department will become involved. In smaller companies it might be the owner of the company

- Once the profile and ad is written and approved, the advertisement is placed (or placement companies or headhunters are enlisted).

- Resumes come in and the screening and selection process begins.

- Phone interviews help with the selection process and to set up the first round interviews. After this, the second round of interviews help further the selection process.

- Between the second and third round (or final) interviews, 'internal selling' begins. The department manager, hiring manager and others who will be working with the possible new hire begin selling each other on the different candidates. If you are not sure what this means watch the judges on shows like American Idol. Each person has their own idea of what's best and what's needed.

- From there, the third or final interview takes place. The managers meet, discuss options and the single candidate is selected.

- The Job Offer.

- Acceptance of the Job Offer.

- New Hire joins the Company.

- The Probationary Period.

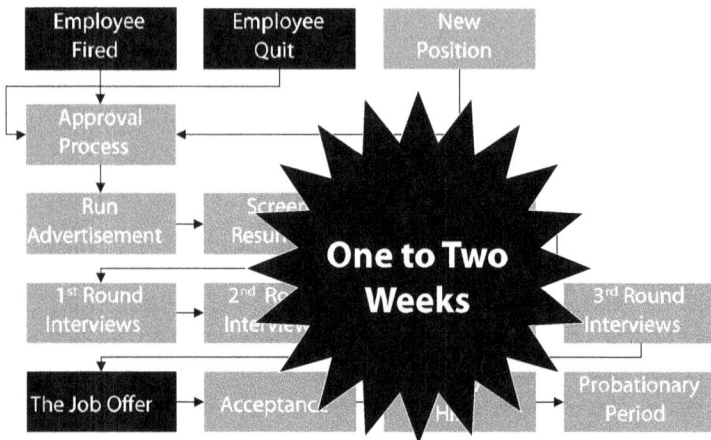

All of this happens in 1-2 weeks. When you apply for a position, getting in and following up need to be done with a sense of urgency. The example that we're using is a 3-interview process, but sometimes there are only one or two. There are employers who will schedule a series of interviews and hire the right one on the spot. These situations make the length of time even less.

Because of the high number of people applying for the same job, it's easy for a hiring manager to be overwhelmed. The typical ad on Craigslist can yield 500, even a 1000 or more resumes depending on what city you are in.

1000 resumes give the hiring manager a lot of choices but here can be too much of a good thing. It's frustrating and daunting to have this many candidates.

The hiring manager wants to get someone hired and trained in a minimum amount of time, all the while finding the best person for the company. Every day that the position remains unfilled, the company is losing productivity, not only from the open position but from the involved people not doing their jobs.

Once the resumes start pouring in, they begin the 'sort.'

In my web ads, I tell people to enclose their resume in the body of the e-mail. I also mention that I will NOT open any attachments. I do this for two reasons: to see who is computer savvy enough to do this and still have their resume look good and to see who is going to follow directions. A lot of hiring managers do the same thing. Creating simple rules will completely take a candidate out of the running. No matter how good your job history, if you can't follow directions, your resume will not get read. This removes approximately 30% of the resumes. Poorly formatted resumes that are hard to read remove another 10-15%.

Then, there is PROXIMITY. Many hiring managers delete candidates who are not in the general area, since they want to make sure that they can get to the office on time, everyday. This removes another half or more of the resumes. Usually, this stack becomes the B-List in case they need to expand the search.

Next is relevance, clarity and the 'Wow' Factor. Is the resume, experience and aptitude appropriate for the job posted? Does the candidate make clear, concise statements about their abilities and background? Finally, does the candidate demonstrate Aptitude, Attitude and Appetite? How do they into THEIR value proposition?

Foolish "cut and paste" mistakes will keep the applicant from being called. Hiring Managers don't want to think that you are applying for every position in the area. It's important to make the recipient of your resume feel special and unique, it also makes them feel like you have taken the extra time to communicate with them.

I know that some of you may be thinking that this is harsh. It may be, and some of it leans toward unfair hiring practices, but it is done every day, everywhere. Businesses are looking for the "best-of-the-best" to add to their company's success and strengths. Businesses want valuable employees who are in top 1-5% of their industry.

After all of the sorting and selecting, the resumes are now a manageable number. The resumes are now scrutinized so there can be a manageable number of first round candidates, who will be interviewed by phone or in person.

THEM: Their Value Proposition

YOU: The 3-As
(attitude, aptitude and appetite)

Remember the Pareto principle? The top 20% of the candidates will be more qualified than all of the others who apply. Out of 1000 resumes, it's possible that they have narrowed it down to 200, then reviewed the stack and narrowed to 40 and once again to an initial group of 8-10. Where would you fit in that stack?

At this point in time, the interviewer is fully committed to interviewing as many people as they must in order to find someone who meets or exceeds the expectations of their company, someone who will add to the corporate DNA and someone who is a good fit. They start with the first round candidates knowing that they may need to go back to the stack.

When I look at resumes, the first things I look at are verbs – the action words that tell me if someone is results oriented.

I also look for someone who demonstrates the 3 As and whether they understand that their actions and abilities will lead to profitability in the form of additional sales, better processes, and cost savings.

The real value proposition is how you take your Attitude, Aptitude and Appetite and help the reader draw a conclusion that you will help their company to improve in some way and to increase profits.

There also needs to be a clearly stated objective, an easy-to-read, easy-to-understand resume with a pattern of success.

THEM: Their Value Proposition

Profitability

YOU: The 3-As
(attitude, aptitude and appetite)

Your Attitude, Aptitude and Appetite must fit into THEIR value proposition.

The value proposition is always the same although it may be stated differently from company to company, but it always comes down to the same thing...they want a profitable business, giving them enough money to give their shareholders a good salary, pay their suppliers and employees and have money left over to grow their business.

The things that will add to the success of any department or company are:
- Increased revenue or throughput
- Improved customer relations
- Added Revenue
- Sold $xx.xx
- Reduced costs
- Saved money
- Produced <<xx>> two times faster than....

This is very simple: give them a reason to hire you. Let them know that if hired, you will add to their profitability.

If you don't really honestly care about helping them, why should they care about hiring you?

The Resume

The resume is your primary marketing tool. Your interview is your presentation and you are seeking to make the sale. The resume is a tool for you to obtain an interview...not a tool to get the job

You are the brand that you are trying to sell. Market yourself through your resume and let the future employer know your features and benefits. What are your strengths? What makes you unique? Why do you stand out from everyone else?

Strive to be clear and concise. The purpose of your resume is to generate enough interest so an employer will contact you for an interview. Use the interview to provide a more detailed explanation of your accomplishments and land a job offer.

Your resume is an example of your communication style and organizational skills.

Employers appreciate a well prepared resume and will use this as a gauge to determine the type of employee you will be. Conversely, a sloppily produced resume is a terrific way to have you removed from the process.

In the body of your resume, be concise - use bullets with short sentences. A resume is typically scanned inside of 30-60 seconds, so make it easy to read.

Use action words. Indicate to the hiring manager that you will add to the organization. Show how you will add profits, revenue and productivity. Whether you are in sales, operations, production, front office, clerical or facilities, there are ways that you can demonstrate this. A sample list is provided in this book.

1. Use Numbers, Dollars and Percentages. These stand out in the body of a resume and indicate quantifiable measurements.

   - Was responsible for cost containment in my department resulting in $250,000 savings.

   - Increased sales by 30% in a 15-state territory.

- Was in the Top 5 of 300 sales reps consistently

2. Lead with your strengths and include transferable skills

3. Problem Solving. Most professional jobs require that you can solve problems utilizing intuition and analytical skills.

4. Decision Making Skills

5. Teamwork

6. Relationship Building inside and outside of the organization

7. Communication

8. Leadership

Construct your resume so it's easy to read.. Leave white space and use a font size no smaller than 10 point. Limit the length of your resume to 1-2 pages.

Have someone proofread your resume. Ask for feedback and have it checked for grammar, punctuation and spelling. Have someone review your career objective. Make sure that the resume is interesting and does not lead the reader to say, "So what?"

All in all, be brief. Pick your strengths and achievements and highlight those so you can achieve your single objective at this point…the interview.

A resume is a one or two page brief summary of your skills, experience, and education and should include:

NAME & ADDRESS
Record your full name and your main home address. Provide a phone number where you can be reached at all times with area codes. If you have an e-mail address write it down. If you put your cell phone number down as a way of reaching you, preface it with cell: (555)-555-1234. I get frustrated when I call someone and they have a lousy phone or phone service. Letting them know that they are calling a cell phone will manage to expectations and will explain, in advance, the possibility of dropped calls, background noise and poor signal.

OBJECTIVES
Some sample objectives are listed on page_____. The right use of objectives is a way for the prospective employer to quickly match a resume for relevance.

EXPERIENCE AND CAREER HISTORY
Reverse chronological order (most recent position first) is easier to understand for the reader. List all of your jobs, paid or volunteer, full time or part time. Use a yearly format (1999-2003 or 2001-present). Indicate skills used or gained and Employer Details, Job Title and Responsibilities or Tasks

AWARDS
Include professional, work-related and civic awards. This can range from a Toastmaster's Award to Most Valuable Volunteer at an animal shelter. List areas of special recognition.

EDUCATION
No one cares what elementary or middle school you attended. If you did not go to college and you are under 24 or 25, list your high school. Once you are in your mid- to late 20s and if you have further education, list your college or university and field of study and degree. Also include certificates, training courses and professional or occupational qualifications.

INTERESTS/ACTIVITIES
These are optional categories on your resume. This is your chance to show your personal values. Include social or civic activities, sports, fitness, and hobbies. Stay away from religion. This is your chance to introduce a human element into your resume.

MISCELLANEOUS
Anything else that you feel important

REFERENCES
Do not list references on your resume. Write that your references are "Available upon request." Prepare a separate list of professional references (3-5), including name, title, address, and business phone number of each person who agreed to be a reference for you.

Chronological vs. Functional

Functional resumes have skills grouped in categories at the beginning and past job titles at the end. This format is for those who have had huge gaps in employment, have changed jobs many times or have not had a consistent career path in the same industry. The functional resume is a way of highlighting your transferable skills. If you are going to use a functional resume format, know that most employers expect to see a chronological resume so it is very important to demonstrate some tremendous abilities.

Chronological resumes list each job along with duties and highlights in reverse chronological order. When organizing a chronological resume, you outline sections of your experience, education, and skills to communicate what you have accomplished.
Avoid Resume Mistakes

1. Always have dates.
2. List Features and benefits
3. Never list the reasons you left your job. Never mention something that would cause an eyebrow to be raised: a lawsuit, sexual harassment, a Worker's Compensation claim or being fired without cause.
4. Don't include personal information. Do not mention your age, race, creed, or gender.
5. Your resume should not be more than two pages.
6. Looks count! Keep the resume in 10-12 pt type. No fancy fonts and no strange colors. White or off-white paper is still the best and your second page and mailing envelope should match.
7. Don't forget to add an objective.
8. Don't lie or change dates to fill in gaps. Do not do it. This is extremely easy for people to uncover.

Many of the larger employers are using Resume Scanning as a method of storing and searching resumes. If you know that your resume is going to be scanned, the following are recommendations:

- Do not use bold print, italics, or underlining.
- Use a clear typestyle. (10, 11 or 12pt)
- Leave large margins on all sides of the resume. (1" is good)
- Only use white or very light ivory paper.
- Be sure to center your name, address and telephone at the top.

Sample Resume

Bill Jackson
1234 Village Parkway
San Ramon, CA 94556
Phone: 1.510.555.1345 Cell:1.510.555.2299
email: bill.jackson@email.com

OBJECTIVE:
I am seeking a position as a Marketing Research and Strategy Professional with a Fortune 200 company allowing me to use my creative and analytical skills resulting in increased market share, sales and profits.

SUMMARY OF QUALIFICATIONS:
- Excellent research, business modeling and analytical skills.
- Superb presentation and writing skills proven through consulting and research.
- Exceptional project management skills with keen attention to detail.
- Strong consensus building ability.
- Proven ability to manage client relationships.
- Vertical Market, Competitive Analysis and Product Positioning
- Vertical Market Analysis

PROFESSIONAL EXPERIENCE
Acubine, Berkeley, CA – 2010 - Present
- Product and Marketing Manager
- Directed a very successful product launch campaign in the European market.
- Designed and led well-received executive presentations to national distribution channels.
- Expanded sales education through research and compilation of product, market and competitive information.
- Established a regular sales information update process. These changes led to 30% reduction in time spent in accessing information.

BalanceLine, Inc., Fremont, CA – 2004 - 2010
Senior Consultant (2006-2008)
Consultant (2004-2006)
- Promotion due to exceptionally high quality of deliverables and for surpassing targets.
- Exceeded sales targets by 200%, 25%, and 100% respectively in three consecutive years.
- Developed strategic relationships with several large Global 1000 companies.
- Consistently delivered projects on time and under budget.
- Evaluated competitive market trends and developed product positioning strategies for a Global 100 communication systems provider. Study involved

4Ps (Product, Price, Promotion, Place) and SWOT (Strengths, Weaknesses, Opportunities, Threats) analyses.

- Developed competitive product positioning for business process outsourcing and online banking offerings of a Fortune 1000 financial solutions provider. As a result, the company differentiated its product bundles and was able to increase market penetration by more than 1000%.
- Facilitated comprehensive customer needs assessment for supply chain management and customer relationship management solutions in the wholesale distribution market for a Fortune 1000 software provider. Study involved quantitative survey and gap analysis. Based on the results, the client refocused its product development efforts to better meet customer requirements.
- Determined strategic market opportunities and helped to re-channel more than $200 million dollars of investment into high growth areas for a data center outsourcing provider.

Raytag Freiden, San Francisco, CA -- 2004
Research Analyst
- Devised innovative research strategies and business models to provide the first ever company forecast on the use of e-commerce as a channel by biotech companies.

EDUCATION
- M.A., International Economics, University of California, Berkeley, CA.
- B.A., Economics, Cal State Hayward, Hayward, CA, (GPA 3.82)

AWARDS
- Team Award for Excellence in Customer Satisfaction, 2004 - Managed a major project that was awarded Team Award for Excellence in Customer Satisfaction.
- CMT - Toastmaster's International

PROFESSIONAL/CIVIC AFFILIATIONS
- American Management Association
- Toastmaster's International
- Elk's Club

COMPUTER SKILLS
- Microsoft Access
- Microsoft Excel
- Microsoft Power Point
- Microsoft Word
- Microsoft Visio
- ACT
- Goldmine

REFERENCES ON REQUEST

Employment Objectives

It is very important to relate your objective to the reader.

What is it that will compel the person who is reading your resume to want to interview you and hire you?

Read and reread these, and then take the time to write your objective. Your objective will be your mission statement.

Sample Strong Objectives

- To use my computer science skills and training in software development for designing and implementing operating systems.

- A marketing position which will maximize opportunities to develop and implement programs, to organize people and events, and to help perpetuate the branding identity resulting in additional sales.

- A position as an Account Manager with a commercial printing company which will utilize my print and sales skills and knowledge resulting in additional business. Long term goal: Sales Management.

- A position in data analysis where skills in mathematics, computer programming, and deductive reasoning will contribute to new systems development.

- Retail Management position which will use my sales/customer service experience and people skills to develop a winning team leading to an increase in sales growth. Long term goal: Progression to regional manager.

- Working in an organization which is fully operational and adhering to their strategic plan.

- Making improvements in processes, customer service and carrying out the overall goals of the organization for joint success.

- To utilize my computer skills and customer service attributes to the fullest level, while having a positive impact on the employer's system environment.

- A Human Resources or Administrative position where my skills can be effectively utilized to improve operations and contribute to company profits.

- With over 12 years of broad and versatile experience in Technical Writing for the Regulated, Marketing, and Software environments, I am professionally skilled in document creation, editing, archiving, and management.

- Finance professional with excellent business skills and diversified experience in accounting, planning, analyses, systems and management. A highly motivated team player who takes initiative and interfaces effectively with all levels within the organization and a management style that encourages independent judgment with follow-through.

Poor Objectives

- To work in a team environment where I may learn additional skills.

- Management position which will use my experience and will provide opportunities for rapid advancement.

- A position in social services which will allow me to work with people in a helping capacity.

- A position in Personnel Administration with a progressive firm.

- Sales Representative with opportunity for advancement.

- A position as Help Desk Analyst, Technical Support

- A job as a driver.

- A challenging position as an Electronic Engineer or Engineering Technician with a dynamic company.

- To help your company grow

Accomplishments

A basic sales process is to discuss features and benefits. The 'Feature' is the specifications of the product. The 'Benefit' is how the performance of the product will benefit the user. A feature of a remote control for a television would be the group of buttons. The benefit is not needing to get up from the couch. An employer wants "the what, how, where, and when" you used your skills. They want to hear how your features will benefit them and how you excelled in your performance and how your accomplishments set you apart from the other candidates. Remember, if there is only one job and there are hundreds or thousands of applicants, you have to be the best fit.

Take out a sheet of paper and list your accomplishments. Include all business-related successes in your life. Include your accomplishments from past employment or learning activities. Include the metrics: how did you improve, meet a challenge, increase throughput, saved time or money. These may have been from your own effort or as part of a team. When stating your accomplishments, use numbers or percentages whenever possible.

- Successfully managed $4.5mm in accounts receivables and reduced delinquent accounts by 15 percent.

- Participated on a fund-raising team for the Elks Club that raised $35,000 for youth programs.

- Reviewed grant applications to award over $17 million in funds to supportive housing programs throughout the state.

- Achieved 205% of fiscal year 2003 budget, $2.4M, while managing national Travel and Transportation vertical market.

- Identified, researched and recommended a new phone provider resulting in saving the company's costs by 22 percent.

- Crafted donor letters that resulted in more than $105,000 in donations year to date.

- Over 5 years experience driving and delivering in heavy city traffic, with a perfect driving record saving current company down-time and insurance premiums.

- More that twenty years experience in customer service and print production.

- Natural problem solving skills that create both practical and agreeable solutions.

- Bilingual in English and Spanish allowing for seamless customer service while working with Spanish-speaking customers.

- Typing speed: 70+ words per minute resulting in higher on-time reports than peers

- Responsible for twice-monthly payroll activities, ensuring that employees were paid as expected and on time

- Suggested and implemented new processes that reduced customer phone time by 5 minutes per order and increased time for upselling resulting in a 10% increase in sales.

- Experience in teaching, group presentations (up to 35 persons) and workshops.

Action Words

As you begin to develop your resume, cover letter, and prospectus letter and you begin to work on your cold-calling and interviewing skills, painting a picture is very important. Here are several pages of words that will help to paint a picture of your skills and abilities.

A

accelerated
accomplished
achieved
acquired
acted
adapted
added
adjusted
administered
adopted
advanced
advertised
advised
advocated
affected
aided
aired
allocated
altered
amended
amplified
analyzed
answered
anticipated
appointed
appraised
approached
approved
arbitrated
arranged
ascertained
assembled
assessed
assigned
assisted
attained
attracted
audited
augmented
authored
authorized
automated
availed
awarded

B

balanced
bargained
borrowed
bought
broadened
budgeted
built

C

calculated
called
canvassed
capitalized
captured
carried out
cast
cataloged
centralized
chaired
challenged
changed
channeled
charted
checked
chose
circulated
clarified
classified
cleared
closed
co-authored
cold-called
collaborated
collected
combined
commissioned
committed
communicated
compiled
completed
complied
composed
computed
conceived
conceptualized
concluded
condensed
conducted
conferred
consolidated
constructed
consulted
contracted
contributed
controlled
converted
convinced
coordinated
corrected

corresponded
counseled
counted
created
critiqued
cultivated
cut

D

debugged
decentralized
decided
decreased
deferred
defined
delegated
delivered
demonstrated
depreciated
described
designated
designed
determined
developed
devised
devoted
diagrammed
directed
directing
disclosed
discounted
discovered
dispatched
displayed
dissembled
distinguished
distributed
diversified
divested
documented
doubled
drafted

E

earned
eased
edited
effected
elected
eliminated
employed
enabled
encouraged
endorsed
enforced
engaged
engineered
enhanced
enlarged
enriched
entered
entertained
established
estimated
evaluated
examined
exceeded
exchanged
executed
exercised
expanded
expedited
experience
explained
exposed
extended
extracted
extrapolated

F

facilitated
familiarized
fashioned
fielded
figured
financed

focused
forecasted
formalized
formed
formulated
fortified
found
founded
framed
fulfilled

G

gathered
governed
grouped
guided

H-I

hired
identified
implemented
improved
increased
informed
initiated
innovated
inquired
inspected
inspired
installed
instigated
instilled
instituted
instructed
insured
interfaced
interpreted
interviewed
introduced
invented
inventoried
invested
investigated

invited
involved
isolated
issued
issued

J-K-L
joined
judged
launched
lead
lectured
led
lightened
liquidated
litigated
lobbied
localized
located

M
maintained
managed
mapped
marketed
maximized
measured
mediated
merchandised
merged
met
minimized
modeled
moderated
modernized
modified
monitored
motivated
moved
multiplied

N
named

narrated
negotiated
noticed
nurtured

O
observed
obtained
offered
offset
opened
operated
operationalized
orchestrated
ordered
organized
oriented
originated
overhauled
oversaw

P
participated
passed
patterned
penalized
perceived
performed
permitted
persuaded
phased
pinpointed
pioneered
placed
planned
polled
positive
prepared
presented
preserved
presided
prevented
priced

printed
prioritized
probed
processed
procured
produced
proficient
profiled
profitable
programmed
projected
promoted
proved

Q-R
qualified
quoted
raised
ranked
reacted
read
received
reconciled
recorded
recovered
rectified
redesigned
reduced
refined
regained
regulated
reinforced
reinstated
rejected
remedied
remodeled
renegotiated
reorganized
repaired
replaced
reported
represented
requested

researched
resolved
resourceful
revealed
revitalized

S
safeguarded
salvaged
saved
scheduled
screened
secured
segmented
selected
sent
separated
served
serviced
settled
shaped
shortened
showed
shrank
signed
simplified
sold
solved
spearheaded
specialized
specified
speculated

spoke
spread
stabilized
staffed
staged
standardized
steered
stimulated
strategized
streamlined
strengthened
stressed
substantiated
successful
superseded
supervised
surpassed
systematized

T
tabulated
tailored
targeted
taught
terminated
tested
testified
tightened
traced
traded
trained
transacted

transferred
transformed
translated
transported
traveled
treated
tripled

U
uncovered
undertook
unified
united
updated
upgraded
used
utilized

V
validated
valued
verified
versatile
viewed
visited

W-X-Y-Z
weighed
welcomed
widened
willing
wrote

Assembling your Resume

Now that we have gone through the components of the resume, here is a worksheet to help you assemble your thoughts and to help you stay focused.

Heading: First Name, Middle Initial, Last Name:

_____

Street Address, Apt. Number, City, State, Zip:

_____

Area Code and Phone Number:

_____

E-mail Address:

_____

Objective (always best to name the position or related positions that you are seeking:

_____

_____

_____

Education - Year completed, School Name, City, State, GPA/ List areas of study:

Skills:

_____

_____

_____

_____

_____

Transferable skills and examples of how you have used them:

_____

_____

_____

Work History - Dates of employment, duration, title, employer, job description and 3-4 key responsibilities (and successes):

_____

_____

_____

_____

_____

_____

Honors and Awards:

_____

_____

_____

Clubs and Organizations:

_____

_____

_____

Hobbies (if applicable):

_____

_____

_____

The Cover Letter

Your cover letter is your chance to make a great first impression and to further personalize the information that is contained in your resume. This is your chance to present your goals, qualifications and availability to a prospective employer in a clean, appealing and succinct format.

You can refer to the major highlights in your resume as well as explain any gaps in employment. Never include negative information in your cover letter and NEVER bad-mouth former employers.

If you found yourself in a situation where your employment was terminated and you used this time to go back to school in preparation for a career change, this is the place to mention that you have these new skills.

Cover Letter Tips:

1. Address your cover letter to a specific person. Do some research to find the name of the hiring manager (or the person doing the research).

2. Customize your cover letter to the particular job to which you are applying.

3. DO your homework. What do you like about the company?

4. How will you fit? Show your desire and abilities.

5. Do not repeat your resume – Highlight but do not repeat.

6. Spell check and grammar check.

7. A traditional look is best. Use an easy to read typeface - 10 point or above - and close the letter with Sincerely, Sincerely Yours or Cordially. Do not forget to sign it!

The Prospectus Letter

If you call and ask the Human Resource Department what jobs are available, you will get a clear, concise response outlining the jobs that are available and nothing more. Human Resources will get involved only when an actual identified job exists.

The primary objective of a department manager has always been to grow profitable business and find ways to improve systems and processes.

If a qualified candidate comes along who can help them achieve their initiatives, they will take the time to meet with those people and, if they are compelling, will hire them.

So, how do you do it?

Simple, do not send your resume. Instead, send a brief prospectus to the president, VP or department manager at the company and sell them on the idea of meeting with you.

The three things that attract them to an employee or prospective employee are Attitude, Aptitude and Appetite. Receiving a prospectus like this is a way for the prospective employee to demonstrate all of these factors.

Take some time to look at all of the information on the company website, look at competitive websites, and talk to people in the organization.

Use your experience to provide insights. Explain in your letter what your skills and abilities are and how you can contribute to the success of the organization

Then.... do not email it.

An email can de deleted too quickly. Send this express mail, by standard mail in a 9x12 envelope, or deliver it in person.

Make it look as important to them as it is to you.

When you send a prospectus letter, you are creating your own position. This position is one that has not been posted and the Human Resources does not know about it, so there is no competition.

Responding to Internet Ads

Understand style implications. Use normal upper and lower case letters. Do not use ALL CAPS. In computer communications, all caps mean that you are shouting. Additionally, it is hard to read and it makes you look like you do not have computer skills.

Respond appropriately. If they ask for resumes by mail, send it by mail. If they ask for a resume by e-mail, e-mail it to them.

While most people do not object to your being clever it's always best to follow the instructions. Whatever you do, do not e-mail a link to your website that contains your resume.

Be specific. Identify the position that you are applying for along with your objective.

Do not make the hiring manager figure out what you want.

Keep your cover letter brief, concise and factual.

Do not repeat what you have in the resume. It can be a good idea, however, to make a reference to something that will tie in to the job that you are applying for.

Script Writing and Cold Calls

When you start calling prospective employers, be prepared for a preliminary interview over the telephone. Write down some of the answers that may be asked of you regarding your experience, about yourself and what you are looking for in a job.

When the receptionist answers, say "Hello, My name is <first and last name> and I'm calling for the <office/sales/marketing/IT> manager."

If the receptionist asks what this is regarding, you can take one of two roads. My preference is to warm up to the receptionist and get them to work with you as a coach. The other road is to tell them that the call is of a personal nature and that you would prefer to either speak to the person directly or to be transferred to their voicemail.

The next line using the first approach is "I am looking for work as a <<bookkeeper/account manager/customer service rep>>. I've recently discovered your company and feel that my experience would lend itself to success with the <<ABC Company>>. If you can provide me with the department manager's name and connect me, I'd really appreciate it."

Most times, the receptionist will work with you. If you feel that you are on a roll, this is a good time to verify the address of the company and get the e-mail address of the hiring manager.

Once you've been connected to the hiring (department) manager, you are 'on'.

Begin with an introduction. "Hello Mr. Jones, I'm Joe Smith."

It is important to sound confident, professional and enthusiastic and equally important not to overdo it.

Now tell them what your specialty is along with a couple of key strengths. Use the information that you put together from your resume objective: "Mr. Jones, I'm looking for a retail management position that will use my sales and customer service experience along with my people skills. I have 10 years of experience developing winning teams. I feel this expertise will lead to an increase in sales growth for the XYZ Company. I'd like to springboard my success in that position to ultimately being a District Manager."

Then ask the question.

"When is a good time for me to come in for an interview?"

This is an open-ended question that requires an affirmative answer and shows your appetite for the job. DO NOT ask IF you can come in for an interview. This is a close-ended question that will result in your getting a "NO."

In this book, there are a series of interview questions...be prepared for these. It is very possible that the hiring manager will take this as an opportunity to interview you on the spot. Have the interview questions written on 3x5 cards and be ready.

Once you have your script written, you will want to speak directly with the hiring managers. You can find these people in several sources: Hoover's Online, Rich's Guide (Norcal Directories), cold-calling, etc. (Rich's Guides can be found in the business section of your main library).

Put the information that you get from these different sources on a 3x5 card. This will become your database.

Telephone Tips

- Straighten up your desk – get rid of clutter. Reducing clutter helps you to stay focused

- Have your vision board nearby. This is your oasis. This is what you will be looking at to recharge yourself and keep you motivated.

- Smile when you talk on the phone. Yes, it sounds crazy because the other person cannot see you, but a smile does carry over into your voice.

- Sound enthusiastic and upbeat.

- Do not to make any negative comments, especially about yourself.

- Practice your cold-calling techniques with friends or family.

- Keep revising and improving your script.

- Avoid using slang or corporate buzzwords.

- Your voice and manner of speaking should be relaxed but professional.

- Have a copy of your resume in front of you so you can refer to it in case they ask questions.

- If you are met with rudeness or negativity, do not take it personally. The person you are talking to may be having a bad day (Be sure you are not calling a company that has specified 'no calls' in their ad).

- If they say there are no job openings, ask if they can refer you to other departments or companies that may be hiring.

- If you do not get an interview, but do get information (the name and number of a hiring manager, an estimated time a job may open up, etc.), then count it as a success and write it down so you can follow up on it later.

- Do not expect them to call you back -- it is your job to call them back. If they say there are no openings at present, ask if you can call back in a few weeks to see what's happening.

- Always be polite and say thank you. The person you're speaking to may have a say in whether you will be called in for an interview.

- Do not talk too fast or too much.

Getting Ready for the Interview

You put together your resume and sent them out. You posted your resume on job sites. You called everyone you know to let them know that you are looking for a job. You are networking and searched on the web in order to send out the prospectus letters and now, you have a few people calling you back.

Let's impress these folks and make this a memorable interview for them and for you.

- Know your resume backwards and forwards. This is something you control 100% - memorize it, know the dates of each job. Have a friend or family member quiz you on the information in the resume. If the interviewer asks you a question about an item on the resume and you stumble, it'll make you look forgetful or that you made up the information.

- Have answers ready for the frequently asked questions on the next several pages.

- Do practice interviews with friends and in front of the mirror.

- Begin with a web search on www.google.com See where and how the company shows up in the search.

- Find their website and news about the company. Look at every page of the company's website. Take Notes. Get a feel for the company's direction. Read press releases; look over Standard and Poor and the corporate records. Have there been any unusual changes in their organization, any new products and services, large increases or decreases in sales?

- For smaller companies, call the local Chamber of Commerce. Get the company's annual report from its website, if available.

- Visit their website to read about the direction of the company and any current media coverage.

- Arrive at least 10 minutes early. Be prepared for heavy traffic and for errors with your GPS, Google, Yahoo Maps or Mapquest.

- Dress appropriately. Try to find a coach in the company where you are applying. Find out what the dress code is and wear clothing one notch above the dress code.

If you learn that the dress code is jeans and collared shirts, dress business casual. If it is business casual, wear slacks and a sports coat. If the dress code is more traditional - a dress shirt and slacks - wear a suit. If the dress code is a suit, wear my best suit.

If you are applying for a sales position, odds are that you'll wear a suit. If you are applying for a warehouse management position, more than likely you'll be in business casual. When in doubt, wear a suit or sports coat with color coordinated pants, a dress shirt, and a tie. For women: wear a classic suit or a simple dress with a jacket. This is not the time to be provocative or sexy. Some appropriate colors are navy blue, black, or gray.

Look neat and clean!
Look in the mirror. Hair (facial and head) should be styled appropriately. This is not the time to wear wild styles. If that's your personal style and you think that it is important, do it on a second or third interview. If getting a job is more important than a personal fashion statement, aim for the more traditional, conservative look.

Perfume and Cologne
Don't do it. Many people have allergies and heavy scents set them off.

Tattoos and piercings
Although tattoos are somewhat mainstream, people who have tattoos on their hands, forearms or in other visible areas are flirting with danger in the job market.

There are many people who are closed-minded about tattoos and piercings and will be put off by visible tattoos. This is also a bad time to wear nose, lip, eyebrow or an excessive number of earrings.

Shoes and Socks
Men: wear matching socks.
Women: wear hosiery.
Shoes should be leather, Black or cordovan are best. Make sure they are clean and polished.

The Handshake

This is a very telling way to understand the person you are meeting. Do you come from the top and give the power handshake? Do you shake hands very lightly?

These examples may seem simple, but it is easy to start off poorly with a bad handshake.

Avoid the light delicate handshake and the powerful over-the-top controlling handshake. Give a firm, full-handed handshake with members of both sexes.

Posture

Body language tells a story about you. Your body posture, how you sit and facial expressions speak volumes to your potential employer. A slight lean forward when you are speaking is good.

Listen carefully during the interview.

You have a lot on your mind and quite often, nervous people tend to talk excessively.
Resist the temptation to do so. Aside from asking a few direct questions, most of your time should be used to observe your prospective manager.

Pay attention to their manner of speech. Listen carefully how they phrase their comments and the answers to your questions. Are you receiving solid information or vague responses? You will gain much more information by listening than by talking.

Be bold

If you are not clear about the information you receive, politely ask for clarification. Most good managers will appreciate your honesty. It will also show your interest in the company and your new position.

Commonly Asked Questions

Being prepared for an interview is essential to put yourself above the competition.

Having some knowledge about what the interviewer(s) will ask and knowing how to respond to these questions will help you get a second interview and possibly the position.

Practice answering these questions. Make sure you do not sound like you are reading from a script.

How did you prepare for this interview today?

Tell how you researched the company on the Internet. Perhaps you looked at their website, did a Yahoo or Google search, checked up on them through Dun and Bradstreet or another business reference service.

For those companies that are publicly traded, you can get great information on-line through msn.com, e-trade or another financial research engine.

What the hiring manager does not want to hear is that you went out and bought a new outfit or meditated for 30 minutes. Keep it about business.

Tell me about yourself.

This is a very straightforward question that can sometimes lead down the wrong path. Talk about your logical progression. Tell them how you got to this point in your career, what your career goals are as it pertains to their business.

They do not want to know about your husband, wife, kids, your religious convictions or anything of a personal nature. Keep this short and sweet. Stay focused.

What are your greatest strengths?

This is an important question.

Too many people think that they are bragging and they have a hard time with this one. Examples are good, especially if you solved a business problem, streamlined systems and processes and generally added to the organization.

What are your weaknesses?

This question is a killer for most applicants. You should always have more strengths than weaknesses. Have one example to cite and explain how you work on turning it into a strength.

What were your major contributions to your last position? How do you feel you can contribute to this company? How quickly will you be able to contribute to this company?

Cite specific examples of how you positively affected your last company. Relate these to how you can increase productivity for your prospective employer.

How did you help your department?

If you can show you were valuable in your previous positions, it will help the interviewer see that the company can expect the same kind of results from you. You'll want to have a few examples, both quantifiable and qualifiable.

What are your career goals? (Short and Long-Term) How does this position fit into your goals? How does your current skill set fit within these goals? How have your career goals changed over the years?

The interviewer is looking to see how logical you are in your career goals and how you plan on attaining them. If your long-term goal is to be an English teacher and you are applying to become a mailroom manager, odds are that this will be a difficult question to answer.

Ideally, you are making some good job and life choices and there is a logical progression between what you have done, what you are looking at doing now and what your future holds.

What are some of your most significant accomplishments in your past job?—in your career? – Personally?

You should elaborate on some of your key accomplishments that are already on your resume.

How do you work under pressure? What would you consider your management style? What difficulties do you have managing people? How do you handle pressure?

How do you handle several projects at the same time with high deadlines?

The interviewer is trying to see how much work you can handle and how you deal with it. As for turning weaknesses into strengths, you should be as positive as possible. When dealing with weaknesses, always explain the progressions that you have made to improve.

One example: "I had a lot of work on my plate and was unclear of the priorities. I spoke with my manager and he/she clarified my duties in order of importance." This shows you aren't afraid to ask for help and when to ask for it.

How would others describe you? Your colleagues? Your boss? Yourself?

Try to be as honest, yet as positive, as possible. Go back to the chapter on strengths and use some of these words as descriptions.

Do you consider yourself to be a team player?
Do you work well with your colleagues or do you prefer working independently?

As always, being able to work with others is extremely important. Show how you worked within a team and contributed to it.

How do you feel about your current/last position?
What do you like about it?
What do you dislike about it?
Why are you leaving?
How did you feel about your boss?

The interviewer is looking for relevant experiences you have with your current position, including the management style, and how it relates to the position you've applied for.

Talk about your experiences with your duties, how you worked with others, etc.

Although you should always be as honest as possible, stay positive and do not bad-mouth your former employer or boss. Stay objective.

Why should we hire you for this position?
What skills will you bring to this company?
What are your analytical skills?

What are your problem solving skills?
Are you more intuitive or logical?
What computer/equipment skills do you have?

Employers are looking to hire the best candidate for any position.

This person would need to work well within the framework that is already established in the company, as well as show they will work the hardest for them.

Let the interviewer know how you went above and beyond the call of duty in your career.

Focus on your experience, your work ethic, and how you relate to your peers.

What attracted you to our company/the position? What interests you the most?
What interests you the least?
How do you hope to benefit from this company/job?
What characteristics do you think are required for this job?

List the items that you found interesting about the position and the company.

Why are you changing jobs/careers?
What do you look for in a job?
What other positions are you considering?

Potential employers like to know why you're leaving your current position or changing careers. It helps them to determine any risk factors there may be in hiring you. It is important to stay upbeat and positive.

What type of salary would you expect for this type of position?

The salary question is always the touchiest question. There are a couple of schools of thought. Some say that salary shouldn't be discussed at the first interview and if it is brought up, answer in such a way to express that you're finding out about the job and how you might fit within the company. Others say you should know what the salary range is for similar positions within the industry, and if they still want to know what you expect, give them the industry standard range. You should deal with this question in a way that is comfortable for you.

Why were you fired/terminated/let go?

This has to be one of the hardest questions to answer because it usually brings up emotional feelings, or feelings of self-doubt.

If you were fired because of poor performance, you may want to share how you believe that you did the best that you could and that you have spent a lot of time reflecting on how you can be a better employee in the future. If there was a conflict between you and another employee or manager, state in a very matter-of-fact tone that you feel although unfair, it was clear that your services at that company were not a good fit for you or them.

The most important aspect of this is letting the interviewer know that you are a positive person and that you have learned from the experience.

Do You Have Any Questions for Me?

You should always be prepared to ask questions about the company, the position, and/or the industry to show you have done your research.

When you have a chance to interview with the hiring manager, ask, "What is your management style?"

Ask for a tour of the company.

Make mental notes from the tour and look for consistency between these two items. If the manager states that he or she manages in a manner that puts the co-worker first and you notice that no one is smiling or talking to one another, caution is in order here.

Look for things that will help you see if the co-workers are happy. Have they "nested" in their offices, cubicles or workspaces by bringing in personal items? Do they seem happy with where they work? While there could be reasons for the discrepancy between what you hear and what you see, this definitely deserves further qualification.

Trust your intuition and relax.

People tend to spend more time with their co-workers than they do with their families. Even though there is stress in looking for a new job, landing the wrong one can be worse. Would accepting this wrong job decrease your overall happiness?

I had a mentor that used to say, "The horse that wins the race is the one that ran the fastest in the stretch." (The stretch is the last part of the horse race).

After you have outraced all of the other competitors and it is just you and a couple of others in the stretch (the final rounds of the interview process), you are now competing with the best of the best. Unfortunately, there can only be one winner and unlike horse racing, second and third place do not count.

How can you win the race? How can you be the champion? Continue to do your research and be prepared to demonstrate the Three As - Attitude, Aptitude and Appetite.

About the Position
1. Why is the position open?
    a. Is it a newly created position?
    b. If not, why did the last person leave?

2. What is a typical workday like and what would I do?
    a. What are my primary challenges?

3. How are evaluations done?
    a. How often?
    b. How do I get feedback about my performance?

4. What are some of the short-term and long-term goals you would like to see achieved within the position?

5. What would you consider to be a successful employee within this position?

6. What freedom do I have in establishing my own goals and deadlines?

About the Company
1. Is there high employee turnover?

2. How does the company contribute to its employees' professional development? Education?

3. Are you financially stable?

4. What are the company's plans for future growth?

5. How has this company fared during the recent recession?

6. How do industry trends impact this company?

7. What makes your firm different from its competitors?

8. What are the company's strengths and weaknesses?

9. What is the corporate work culture?

About Management
1. How would you describe your management style?

2. What are the goals of the department?

About Career Advancement
1. Does the company promote from within?

2. What is a typical career path for this position?

Questions NOT to Ask at the First Interview

1. Anything that is already answered in the company's literature

2. Anything on the company website

3. What will my salary be?

4. What are the company's benefits packages

5. How do I proceed from here?

6. Should I contact you or will you be in contact?

7. What is the process from here?

8. What would distinguish one potential candidate joining your company from another?

9. How do I prove my commitment to the organization?

Follow Up

You leave the interview and feel good about the position. Now go to your car and write down what just happened. List the topics discussed, the characteristics the interviewer described for the position, and other details. This will help you write a thank you letter that shows both your interest and that you are a perfect match for the position.

Although e-mail thank-you notes are good, consider leaving a voice mail AND then send a traditional thank you card or letter. Follow up by phone a few days later.

Explaining Gaps in your Career

No matter what shape the economy is in, businesses occasionally cut costs by eliminating jobs.

Obviously, the best situation is that you are able to find a job right away. If you cannot, you need to address these gaps as best as you can.

The following (in no particular order) are the best ways to address gaps:

- Independent Contractor – freelancer, journalist, tech writer, substitute teacher

- Education including self-study

- Volunteer Work – Nonprofit Jobs.

- Family duties including medical emergency.

- Independently Wealthy – Travel, Self Improvement

- The other way to work through this is to leave the gap and then explain it during the interview. Whatever you do, do not make things up in your resume. People prefer to hire people who think and work through adversity.

References

When references are called, a good hiring manager will ask as many questions as they can to get a true idea of what your skills are and to if your resume is true. They know to keep the questions legal, however, an experienced person will ask leading questions to get your references to tip them off as to the facts. Remember, they are looking for the best of the best. When I research prospective employees, I do the following:

- I will start off by introducing myself and I will say that you have applied for the position of _____ in our company. I will mention that you listed them or their organization as a reference. I then ask if they will serve as a reference. I will follow up with the comment that this information will remain completely confidential.

- Next I will explain the job in detail (per the job description) and I will ask how they think that you will fit this position.

- I then ask about dates: How long did this person work for the company? Did this person report directly to you? I ask about the job duties performed.

- I will ask about dependability, attendance and ability to work unsupervised.

- I ask if the person demonstrated good judgment, accuracy and team working skills.

- Next I ask about strengths or unique skills and I ask about areas for growth and improvement.

- I close by asking why you left this job and if you would be available for rehire.

You want to increase your chance of a good reference?

- Make sure that salary, dates of hire, promotion and termination are correct.

- Data entry mistakes do take place. Make sure that HR has accurate information.

- Differences in information can be taken as negative indications.

- Keep in touch with your references. Know how to get hold of them, what they are doing now, where they work and what they will say about you. Get their permission and let them know you are using them.

- Know your former employer's policy about references.

Accepting the Job Offer

It is time to celebrate.

After all of your hard work searching and interviewing for a job, you have been offered a position with a company where you really want to work.

You are not done! You have to negotiate wages, and, if you are currently employed, you must neatly sever relations with your exiting employer. Just like the sales cycle that we talked about earlier, this is where you put the price tag on the sale and have the buyer agree. What you are looking for is a win-win. Both sides have to feel good about this and you need to be sure that this new position will fit your financial needs.

First and foremost, it is perfectly okay to tell the person making you the offer that you need a little time to think about it. Obviously, if you are offered exactly what you want, there should be no hesitation in agreeing immediately. If there is some negotiation that comes into play, let the hiring manager know that you need the day or a couple of days to think about it and speak with your spouse or partner. You may also want to talk to other family members, friends or a mentor for feedback.

Be honest in your approach. Do not accept the job over the phone and then later turn it down, as this is a very inconsiderate action. Make sure you completely manage to expectations.

There are several websites that provide detail about salary based on experience and location. Other things to consider in the overall value of the compensation package include signing bonuses, formal or informal training, laptop computers, cell phones, company car or car allowance, medical/dental/life insurance, retirement, profit sharing or deferred earnings, the potential of the position, bonuses and other perks, value of the knowledge that you will be gaining, etc.

Most everyone is uncomfortable with salary negotiation. If you can stay objective in this process you will not only keep a clear head but you will impress your future employer. Staying objective will also keep you from hurriedly accepting the first offer that comes along and keep you from being short-changed in the process. Remember that a difference in $50.00 a week will result in an additional $3,000.00 over five years, and $250.00 a week results in $15,000.00 over five years. These amounts can add up.

Sales and non-sales positions should be negotiated differently. Sales people know that performance-based compensation is more important than base salary. Establishing quotas or goals based on honest potential is important. In addition to these quotas, it is also very important to consider a ramp-up period. You must ask, "How long will it take to build a territory so I can make commissions or bonuses?"

If you are offered a non-sales position you need to take a look at the initial salary and make sure that it meets your financial needs. Do not take the position based on the hope of incremental pay raises. These raises could be based on cost-of-living increases only. It is always best to start with the best package that you can obtain and not rely on the promise of the future.

Earlier in this book, we discussed how the 3As relate to the organization's revenue or profitability. If you can demonstrate how your abilities and knowledge will increase revenue, increase profitability and increase throughput, these are very compelling reasons for the company to give you more money. Focus on what you can do for the company. Demonstrate your value.

If you have two or more offers that can be compared equally, use them as leverage in your negotiation. Be honest because you may need to prove what you say. Always do your negotiations in the manner that gives you the most control and strength. It is better to be face-to-face; however, if you are the type of person who will crumble in person and feel stronger on the phone, by all means do this on the phone. Keep in mind that face-to-face will allow you to better read the other person.

Ask for the terms of your employment and compensation in writing. Some of the items that should be included in this document/letter are:

A clear "we are offering you the job" statement
Conditions of employment (probation, training, drug screening)
Your title and duties
Date and time to report to work
Identification of your immediate supervisor
Salary, benefits and other compensation

If the hiring manager does not provide you with this information, write them a letter confirming what you believe the terms to be and keep a copy for your records.

The Counter-Offer

Don't do it.

If you have already accepted a position with the new company and you renege, you have committed a very unethical and inappropriate act.

If you have decided that it is time to leave your current job, just leave. Do not go back and renegotiate for more money based on what the new company has offered you. If your current employer does not understand your value and if you cannot explain it to them before you start the job search, it is time to go.

Whatever situation was there to make you search for another job will still be there. If you go for a counter-offer and your current employer gives it to you because you are thinking of leaving, you will have a hard time progressing in the company and your current employer will always wonder if you will do it again. If there are future employee cuts, you may be one of them because of their lack of trust.

Working for yourself!

I have worked for myself for the last 10 years, I got frustrated with my last employer and decided that it was time to stop making him money and to do it on my own.

I have a few different things that I do, but the most relevant to this book is one of my current endeavors, Nationwide Barcode (www.nationwidebarcode.com) helps small business get barcodes...the ones that you see on packaging items in stores.

The most important thing about that business is that I am in contact with thousands of people who are starting home-based businesses. I am amazed at the amount of determination and creativity the American people have, even in a down economy. I talk to people who are willing to take a chance and start their own businesses doing what they are best at. I've talked to people who buy and sell on Amazon, import goods from around the world as a distributor, bake cookies or cakes and sell them to small stores, roast coffee, small vineyards, create craft items, fishing lures, write books on items on interest and sell them on the internet. The internet can be big business.

I have several friends who are editors, they work with local businesses and publishers and edit manuscripts. Others who are graphic designers or business consultants, all of whom got tired of working for other people.

My wife is an agent for Univera. She got tired of the Real Estate market and decided to work with people helping them to feel better both physically and financially. There are a lot of good direct marketing companies but it takes finding something relevant, with great company support and leadership. Univera just convinced the former CEO of Avon to come out of retirement to come to work for them as their CEO. That certainly says a lot of the viability of that company.

There are agents making several hundred dollars a month, there are some making tens of thousands a month. Check out her site: Young Mind Body Institute. - http://www.youngbodymindinstitute.com/
Send her an email on the contact page if you want more information.

There are many ways to supplement your income or replace a 9-5 job, but that requires the 3-A's, attitude, aptitude and appetite.

Conclusion

Following this page is the 7-day jump start program and a a few pages of resources.

I hope that you have found this book to be a resource that will help you to find the job that you want. For most of us, our lives are intertwined with our work. It is critical that we find a satisfying job so that we may be balanced in life, love and in work.

I would love to hear from all of you who have read this book. Let me know how you have these ideas and concepts have worked for you.

Write me at phil@mediamediainc.com and let me know.

All the best,

Phil Peretz

The 7 Day Jump-Start Program

For this to work, you have to have the 3As (Attitude, Aptitude and Appetite).

The Attitude and your environment have to be positive, you have to have the right skills and education (Aptitude) and you have to really want to find the job (Appetite).

If you treat your job search as a full time job and devote eight hours a day, five days a week, you will find the job you desire within a very short period of time.

Although you may not be hired in seven days, it is critical that you get your work habits in sync with your situation. Stay focused and stay positive while searching for your new job.

Day One

Focus…your job, is to get a job.

Set up your office or work area at home.

Buy four or five packages of 3x5 cards and a file box. You are going to refer to these often. Although I am extremely computer savvy, I find that it is faster and easier to keep job search materials on cards instead of a database.

Call everyone you know and let them know that you are looking for a job. If you are on Facebook, Twitter or LinkedIn use this as a tool to connect with potential contacts. Ask them if they know anyone who is hiring someone with your experience. It is okay if this activity slides into day two as these could be great contacts for you. Ask your contacts if you can use them a reference. Each referral goes on a separate 3x5 card. Do not call these people yet. Also put the name of the reference on the card.

Decide on a horizontal or a vertical approach to your job search. The horizontal approach is more focused. You want to be an office manager for a high-tech manufacturing company located no more than 45 minutes from home. A vertical approach is broader. You want a job within a 45-minute commute from home that will utilize your computer and bookkeeping skills.

Day Two

Create your resume.

Go to the library or bookstore and read the books about resumes. Go to websites like craigslist.org and look at resumes that have been posted and find resumes that you like. Use them as model resumes for style. Writing a resume should not take any more than 1 day.

Start by creating your resume using a word processing program (Microsoft Word or Works). If you do not have a copy of either of these, you can get Open Office for free. It's Sun Microsystems open source version of Microsoft Office. http://www.openoffice.org/

If you are going to send your document as an attachment, send it as a pdf. All businesses have a copy of Acrobat Reader since it's a free productivity program from Adobe. If you do not have a copy of Adobe Acrobat where you can make a pdf version, there are other programs that will allow you to make a pdf from your document. We recommend this free utility: http://www.cutepdf.com/. Turning your resume into a pdf makes it a cross platform document meaning that anyone can open and print it.

Then, create a text version of your resume

If you do not have any graphic skills, go to a Copy Center and have them set up your resume for you. They can also print 50 copies of your resume and can supply blank second sheets and envelopes.

If you are going to print your resume yourself, go to an office supply store and buy some quality paper with matching envelopes.

While you are there buy an attractive pen and a folio that holds a letter pad. Buy a couple of extra pads of paper and a calendar.

Day Three

Obtain a copy of the last Sunday paper and the employment journal in your area. Identify upcoming job fairs and write these events on your calendar.

Have your interview outfit dry-cleaned, shine your shoes, and put together your interviewing clothes.

Write your cover letter. There is a section on cover letters later in this book. However, if you really want to see some great letters, obtain a copy of *Dynamic Cover Letters Revised* by Katharine Hansen, Randall Hansen Ph.D. This book is published by 10 Speed Press and is available at Barnes and Noble, Borders, etc. Like you did with your resume, write two versions of your cover letter, one for print and one for e-mail.

Write your prospectus letter.

Post your resume on a couple of different websites, but do not overdo it. Most jobs are found through personal connections and not on websites. You are simply covering all your basis.

My favorite sites are www.monster.com, www.craigslist.org and www.hotjobs.com. While you are online, you can set up your job search criteria and have Hotjobs and Monster e-mail you with results on a daily or weekly basis.

Looking for jobs on these websites does several things: You get an idea of what skills are required for your desired job, what types of jobs are available, and which companies are growing.

Day Four

Create a script.

Once you have written your script, you will want to speak directly with the hiring managers. You can find these people in several sources: Hoover's Online, Rich's Guide (Norcal Directories), cold-calling, etc. (Rich's Guides can be found in the business section of your main library). Begin by writing down your "Top 50" employers that fit your skills and desires.

Visit the web sites of the companies that you will be calling. Be sure to visit the web sites of the referrals as well.

Begin calling the referral names on the 3x5 cards.

Begin calling at least 20 of your "Top 50" employers.

Keep detailed notes. Ask for referrals from everyone that you speak with. List the name, main local phone number, and if possible, the Web address

After each call in which you connected with someone, e-mail or mail your resume or prospectus letter, cover letter and/or hand-written thank you note as you deem appropriate.

Day Five

Continue your research on the web for your "Top 50" employers.

Finish calling your "Top 50" employers.

After each call in which you connected with someone, e-mail or mail your resume or prospectus letter, cover letter and/or hand-written thank you note as you deem appropriate.

Review your calls so far for follow up.

Day Six

More Resumes, Cover letters, Thank you notes from the previous day.

Respond to ads in local newspapers, trade publications and on the internet. If the job does not fit your choice of a horizontal or vertical fit, do not waste your time.

If you have previous experience in the job category in which you are seeking employment, consider contacting recruiters (often called Headhunters) and employment agencies. Do not consider agencies that ask for money - the fee should be paid by the employer.

To find an appropriate recruiter, call the Human Resources Department of a target employer and ask, "I'm looking to submit my resume to an employment agency for a (insert type of job) position. When you use a recruiter to find that type of employee, who do you use?"

Executives might find appropriate recruiters in the Directory of Executive Recruiters which is available in most libraries.

Day Seven

Make follow up phone calls to those companies to whom you sent resumes. If you get voice mail, leave a message!

By now you should have several appointments lined up and should have a great deal of activity in the pipeline.

If you are not happy with the results so far, go back to your research and create another "Top 50" list.

Resources

Affirmative Action Register - Publication providing listings of professional, managerial and administrative positions for which qualified candidates are being sought.
http://www.aar-eeo.com/

All Job Search Searches 180 career sites, 500 newspapers, and 300 newsgroups, all in one search.
http://www.alljobsearch.com/

Backpage – similar to Craig's List
www.backpage.com

Bilingual Jobs – Diverse Language Careers
http://www.bilingual-jobs.com/

Blue Steps- Executive Search for senior level positions worldwide
http://www.bluesteps.com/

Career Builder
http://www.careerbuilder.com/

Craigslist - Good place for employer's to find applicants. My guess is that this can be a little frustrating for applicants looking for a job since the response rate for employers is so great. Worth looking at!
http://www.craigslist.org

Flipdog - Website that pulls help wanted opportunities from Corporate Websites.
http://www.flipdog.com/

Hotjobs - One of the best places to find available jobs.
http://www.hotjobs.yahoo.com/

iHispano – Connecting Latinos to great jobs
http://www.ihispano.com/

Indeed.com – searches across all cities/states.
http://www.indeed.com/

Job Central
http://www.jobcentral.com/

JobFox
http://www.jobfox.com/

Monster.com - Another place to find available jobs.
http://www.monster.com

Net-temps (Temporary Jobs)
http://www.net-temps.com/

Simply Hired – Pulls from websites, newspapers, etc.
http://www.simplyhired.com/

Specialty sites

Job Hunt - A complete resource of material ranging from "how-to" to job-search and job-networking resources.
http://www.job-hunt.org

Paycheck City - Great website for paycheck and retirement modeling.
http://www.paycheckcity.com

American Mathematical Society - The American Mathematical Society has an extensive set of resources to help you looking for academic positions and is the premier source for information on careers in mathematics. This includes a list of job postings organized by country and state. In addition, you can sign up for an email service whereby you are automatically emailed all new job postings. Finally, you can submit an electronic c.v. which employers can access, and you can register for the job fairs at the annual AMS meetings.
http://math.ucsd.edu/~sbuss/GradInfo/

Geocities - Links to Job Search Resources for Social Workers.
http://www.geocities.com/capitolhill/9300/

DMOZ - A lot of material, best part are the links to job fairs in all areas.
http://dmoz.org/Business/Employment/Job_Search/

Federally Employed Women - Resource website for Federally Employed Women.
http://www.few.org/job-search.html

Society for Technical Communication – including job resources
http://www.stc.org/

US Museum Employment Resource Center
http://www.museum-employment.com/

Employment resources for Librarians
http://pw1.netcom.com/~feridun/nlintro.htm

Graphic Arts Resource Site
http://wwar.com/employment/

Wetfeet - Company Interviews, Company Profiles, Insider Guides, Salary & Perks Career Profiles, Industry Profiles, City Profiles and more.
http://www.wetfeet.com/asp/home.asp

Job search for Engineers
http://www.interec.net/

Scientists – Job Resources
http://recruit.sciencemag.org/

Government Jobs

Agricultural Research Service
http://www.afm.ars.usda.gov/hrd/

Argonne National Labs
http://www.anl.gov/Careers/index.html

Army Civilian Vacancy Openings
http://cpol.army.mil/

Association of Tennessee Valley Governments
http://www.atvg.org/

Brookhaven National Labs
http://www.bnl.gov/HR/jobs/

Census Bureau
http://www.census.gov/main/www/employop.html

Central Intelligence Agency
https://www.cia.gov/careers/index.html

Commodity Futures Trading Commission
http://www.cftc.gov/aboutthecftc/careers/

Congressional Budget Office
http://www.cbo.gov/Employment/

Consumer Product Safety Commission
http://www.cpsc.gov/about/hr.html

Corporation for National Service

http://www.nationalservice.gov/about/employment/

Defense Logistics Agency
http://www.hr.dla.mil/

Department of Agriculture (USDA)
http://www.usda.gov/da/employ.html

Department of Energy
http://www.doe.gov/about/employment.htm

Department of Health and Human Services
http://www.hhs.gov/careers/index.html

Department of Interior
http://www.doi.gov/hrm/doijobs.html

Department of Justice
http://jobsearch.usajobs.opm.gov/a9dj.asp

Department of Labor
http://www.dol.gov/dol/jobs.htm

Department of State
http://www.state.gov/aboutstatedepartment/

Department of Transportation
http://careers.dot.gov/index.htm

Department of Veterans Administration
http://www.va.gov/jobs/

Department of Defense Human Resources
http://www.dhra.mil/website/index.shtml

Economics Research Service
http://www.ers.usda.gov/abouters/employment/

Environmental Protection Agency
http://www.epa.gov/epahrist/careers/index.html

Federal Aviation Administration
http://jobs.faa.gov/

Federal Bureau of Investigation
http://www.fbijobs.gov/

Federal Bureau of Prisons
http://www.bop.gov/jobs/index.jsp

Federal Communications Commission
http://www.fcc.gov/jobs/

Federal Court Judicial Vacancies
http://www.uscourts.gov/employment.html

Federal Elections Commission
http://www.fec.gov/pages/jobs/jobs.shtml

Federal Emergency Management Agency
http://www.fema.gov/about/

Federal Reserve Bank of Atlanta
http://www.frbatlanta.org/atlantafed/employment/intro_index.cfm

Federal Reserve Bank of Boston
http://www.bos.frb.org/about/employment/index.htm

Federal Reserve Bank of Chicago
http://www.chicagofed.org/about_the_fed/current_job_opportunities.cfm

Federal Reserve Bank of Cleveland
http://www.clevelandfed.org/HR/Index.cfm

Federal Reserve Bank of Dallas
http://dallasfed.org/careers/index.html

Federal Reserve Bank of Kansas City
http://www.kc.frb.org/humanres/careerlinks.htm

Federal Reserve Bank of Minneapolis
http://www.minneapolisfed.org/info/career/

Federal Reserve Bank of New York
http://www.ny.frb.org/careers/index.html

Federal Reserve Bank of Philadelphia
http://www.phil.frb.org/employment/index.html

Federal Reserve Bank of Richmond
http://www.richmondfed.org/about_us/our_jobs/index.cfm

Federal Reserve Bank of San Francisco
http://www.frbsf.org/federalreserve/careers/

Federal Reserve Bank of St. Louis
http://www.stls.frb.org/about/jobsearch.html
Federal Trade Commission
http://www.ftc.gov/ftc/oed/hrmo/jobops.shtm

Government Accountability Office
http://www.gao.gov/careers/index.html

Government Printing Office
http://www.gpo.gov/careers/index.html

International Trade Commission
http://www.usitc.gov/employment/employment.htm

Lawrence Berkeley Lab
http://cjo.lbl.gov/

Lawrence Livermore National Lab
http://jobs.llnl.gov/prod_index.html

Library of Congress
http://www.loc.gov/hr/employment/index.php

National Aeronautics and Space Administration (NASA)
http://www.nasa.gov/about/career/index.html

National Archives and Records Administration
http://www.archives.gov/careers/

National Oceanic and Atmospheric Administration (NOAA)
http://www.noaa.gov/jobs.html

National Park Service
http://www.nps.gov/

National Science Foundation
http://www.nsf.gov/about/career_opps/vacancies/

National Security Agency (NSA)
http://www.nsa.gov/careers/

Office of Management and Budget
http://www.whitehouse.gov/omb/recruitment/index.html

Patent and Trademark Office
http://jobsearch.usajobs.opm.gov/a9pto.asp

Peace Corps
http://www.peacecorps.gov/

Securities and Exchange Commission (SEC)
http://www.sec.gov/asec/secjobs.htm

Smithsonian Institute
http://www.si.edu/ohr/

Associations

American Association of Motor Vehicle Administrators
http://www.aamva.org/

American Association of Port Authorities
http://www.aapa-ports.org/

American Association of State Highway and Transportation Officials
http://www.transportation.org/

American Correctional Association
http://www.aca.org/

American Federation of State, County & Municipal Employees
http://www.afscme.org/

American Legislative Exchange Council
http://www.alec.org/

American Planning Association
http://www.planning.org/

American Public Human Services Association
http://www.aphsa.org/Home/home_news.asp

American Public Transit Association
http://www.apta.com/

American Public Works Association
http://www.apwa.net/

American Society for Public Administration
http://www.aspanet.org/scriptcontent/index.cfm

American Water Works Association
http://www.awwa.org/

Association for Information & Image Management
http://www.aiim.org/

Association of Government Accountants

http://www.agacgfm.org/homepage.aspx

Association of Metropolitan Planning Organizations
http://www.ampo.org/

Association of State & Territorial Health Officials
http://www.astho.org/

City-County Communications and Marketing Association
http://www.3cma.org/

Council for Urban Economic Development
http://www.cued.org/

Council of Development Finance Agencies
http://www.cdfa.net/

Council of State Governments
http://www.csg.org/

Council on Licensure, Enforcement and Regulation
http://www.clearhq.org/

Emergency Information Infrastructure Partnership
http://www.emforum.org/

Environmental Council of the States
http://www.ecos.org/

Federation of Tax Administrators
http://www.taxadmin.org/

Government Finance Officers Association
http://www.gfoa.org/

Institute of Transportation Engineers
http://www.ite.org/

International Association of Assessing Officers
http://www.iaao.org/

International Association of Chiefs of Police
http://www.theiacp.org/

International Association of Crime Analysts
http://www.iaca.net/

International Association of Fire Chiefs
http://www.iafc.org/

International Code Council
http://www.iccsafe.org/

International Economic Development Council
http://www.iedconline.org/

International Institute of Municipal Clerks
http://www.iimc.com

International Public Management Association for Human Resources
http://www.ipma-hr.org/

National Academy of Public Administration
http://www.napawash.org/

National Association of Counties
http://www.napawash.org/

National Association of County & City Health Officials
http://www.naccho.org/

National Association of Development Organizations (NADO)
http://www.nado.org/

National Association of Fleet Administrators
http://www.nafa.org/

National Association of Housing & Redevelopment Officials
http://www.nahro.org/index.cfm

National Association of Local Govt. Environmental Professionals
http://www.nahro.org/index.cfm

National Association of Public Hospitals and Health Systems
http://www.naph.org/

National Association of Regional Councils
http://www.narc.org/

National Association of Regulatory Utility Commissions
http://www.naruc.org/

National Association of State Auditors, Comptrollers and Treasurers
http://www.nasact.org/

National Association of State Budget Officers
http://www.nasbo.org/

National Association of State Chief Information Officers
http://www.nasbo.org/

National Association of State Facilities Administrators
http://www.nasfa.net/

National Association of State Personnel Executives
http://www.naspe.net/

National Association of State Procurement Officials
http://www.naspo.org/

National Association of State Telecommunications Directors
http://www.nastd.org/

National Association of Telecommunications Officers and Advisors
http://www.nastd.org/

National Association of Towns and Townships
http://www.natat.org/

National Center for State Courts
http://www.ncsconline.org/

National Civic League
http://www.ncl.org/

National Community Development Association
http://www.ncdaonline.org/

National Conference of States on Building Codes & Standards
http://www.ncsbcs.org/

National Conferences of State Legislatures
http://www.ncsl.org/

National Environmental Health Association
http://www.neha.org/

National Fire Protection Association
http://www.nfpa.org

National Forum for Black Public Administrators
http://www.nfbpa.org

National Governors Association
http://www.nga.org

National Institute of Governmental Purchasing
http://www.nigp.org/

National League of Cities
http://www.nlc.org/

National Public Employer Labor Relations Association
http://www.npelra.org/

National Purchasing Institute
http://www.nationalpurchasinginstitute.org

National Recreation & Park Association
http://www.nrpa.org/

National Rural Development Partnership
http://www.rurdev.usda.gov/nrdp/

National Sheriffs' Association
http://www.sheriffs.org/

Public Housing Authorities Directors Association
http://www.phada.org

Public Technology Institute
http://pti.nw.dc.us/

State & Territorial Air Pollution Program Administrators
http://www.4cleanair.org/

U.S. Conference of Mayors
http://www.usmayors.org/

Urban & Regional Information Systems Association
http://www.urisa.org/

Urban Land Institute
http://www.uli.org

Western Governors' Association
http://www.westgov.org/

www.ingramcontent.com/pod-product-compliance
Lightning Source LLC
LaVergne TN
LVHW021525080426
835509LV00018B/2670